READY, SET, G☑AL!

THE GEN Z GUIDE TO ACHIEVING MORE

TRISHA B. PEREZ

An Imprint of Storm Praise Publishing

Library of Congress Control Number: 2021932388

ISBN 978-0-9995631-6-8

This is a first edition printing.

Storm Praise Publishing, LLC
Attn: Ready, Set, GOAL! Guide
5668 Fishhawk Crossing Blvd.
Suite 130
Lithia, FL 33547

stormpraisepublishing@gmail.com

www.StormPraise.com

Copyright ©2021 by Trisha B. Perez
Published by Storm Praise Publishing, L.L.C.

For Generation Z

TABLE OF CONTENTS

The Run Down

Think back to the last time you read a book and thought, This book didn't have to be so long, or This idea could have been explained in fewer words. *Ready, Set, GOAL! The Gen Z Guide to Achieving More* is going to be the opposite of that type of book. I understand that a concise message is a strong message. In this guide, the theme is: Get to the point. See below.

In this guide, you will…

> Become a power user of basic life skills by:
> Taking inventory of where you are
> Determining where you want to be
> Designing a vehicle for your journey

What's in a Map?

In this chapter, we will be exploring your big picture map. Before we dig in, we will cover some map basics.

To use a map, we need to know a few basic things:
> Our current location
> Our desired destination
> Directions to our desired destination

Ready, Set, GOAL! The Gen Z Guide to Achieving More will provide you with the knowledge necessary to create the map that will guide you wherever you want to go. By using simple exercises, *Ready, Set, GOAL!* will place you on a path to enjoy lifestyle benefits that mirror the lifestyles of successful people like Sam Walton, Warren Buffet, Jeff Bezos, and Mark Cuban.

If you can open your mind to a state of humility,

you too can enjoy the golden nuggets of wisdom placed all over our world. Sam Walton, the founder of Walmart, said it best in his autobiography, Made in America, "You can learn from everybody." When we practice this truth, we are reminded that even Sam Walton believed that even though he had a lot to teach, he had even more to learn.

Exercise No. 1: Where are you?

What to do:
1. Set a timer for five to ten minutes.
2. Write down where you think you are in life right now. Focus on writing the entire time. Consider all aspects of your life including activities, health, finances, relationships, etc.
3. Stop writing when the timer goes off.
4. Read what you just wrote.

Exercise No. 2: On a perfect day, where would you want to be?

What to do:
1. Set a timer for five to ten minutes.

2. Write down where you would be on a perfect day. Focus on writing the entire time. Consider all aspects of your life including activities, health, finances, relationships, etc.
3. When the timer goes off, stop writing.
4. Read what you just wrote.

So, what is a big picture?

Imagine a big picture hanging over your fireplace for everyone to see. The picture is in a substantial frame. It's not a cheap poster frame but is made of heavy wood that looks expensive and significant. That frame holds a big picture of the perfect day you designed in Exercise No. 2. Your big picture signifies true freedom as defined by your standards.

While one person's perfect day might be lounging on the beach or relaxing with a bunch of friends or family, another person's perfect day might be in a quiet home, soaking in a tub full of warm suds. They are both someone's perfect day, and the existence of one does not affect or negate the other.

What if I told you that this guide can help you have more big picture days more often? Would it be worth the time and money to read to the end of this guide to find out?

Exercise No. 3: Observations

What to do:
1. Set a timer for ten minutes.
2. Write down your observations to the responses to Exercise No. 1 and Exercise No. 2. Try to assess your responses without emotion. When we assess without emotion, we lay a foundation for creating true change. Do your best to separate your assessment from your attachments to people or familiarity, and ask yourself the following questions. Are the people around you pushing you to become the best version of yourself? Are you surrounded by people that are dragging you down to an undesired level? Are you on track to building a life filled with more big picture days? Are there any words that seem to be repeated in your responses? Are those repeated words positive or negative?

William Green, the author of The Great Minds of Investing, interviewed thirty-one different successful investors. Many of those investors spoke about Warren Buffet with awe. Two of those investors were interviewed about their lunch experience with the highly revered entrepreneur. In 2008, Mohnish Pabrai and Guy Spier paid $650,100 for a charity lunch with Warren Buffett. During that three-hour charity lunch, Pabrai and Spier were able to learn from one of the best investors in history. One piece of wisdom that Buffet shared with Pabrai and Spier was to "hang out with people better than you, and you cannot help but improve."

The only way for us to follow Warren Buffet's advice is to first assess our current situation. Where are you right now? Where do you want to be? Identify any obvious factors working against your pursuit of a life filled with big picture days.

Point A

I once lived a life of anxiously teetering on the border between success and mediocrity. I was like a tardy little rabbit—always running late, merely nibbling on the successes I was capable of. Still, to the world, it seemed that I was winning in life more often than not. Inside, however, I was a frantic, unorganized, tired faker who was always securing her wins by a hair.

When speaking about my victories, I wouldn't mention that the price I had paid for success was one enormous pile of neglected, dirty laundry that only increased in size. When visitors complimented me on my tidy home, I failed to mention the pile of random items from the living room that I dumped into my closet just before I let them in.

That is being dishonest—and everybody does that in their own way. I understand that kind of dishonesty. After all, I wanted people to see me as more amazing than I actually was. What I don't understand is why we are dishonest with ourselves. I was unconsciously telling myself that an outward scorecard held a higher value than an internal scorecard. Simply put, I was training myself to look awesome instead of be awesome.

Paradigm Shift from Habit to Intention

Why do we choose to spend our lives like this? Stop and think about that for a moment. Choosing to be dishonest with ourselves is equivalent to choosing to be uncomfortable. Would you want to come inside your home after a long day, complete all of your household obligations, take a shower, put some pajamas on, crawl into your bed, and still have on your socks and shoes? Sounds absurd, doesn't it? Why would anyone choose anything other than the most comfortable option available? Take your shoes off. You're home!

I believe the only reason anyone would make a decision that results in him or her feeling uncomfortable is that he or she does not know a better option is available. Making choices about where we want to go and designing pathways to get there allows for the possibility of a life full of big picture days.

In life, we choose between options laid out for us and options we create for our future. In NLP: The Essential Guide to Neuro-Linguistic Programming, we learn that the greatest advantage in a negotiation is the power to walk away at any time. I believe that we are negotiating every day, multiple times per day. Anything we choose in life is a result of negotiating with ourselves.

Everything comes with terms. In exchange for preparing my husband's lunch and coffee every day, I receive quality time to unwind with him at the end of the day. That's the trade-off.

Another example might be a negotiation with yourself about teaching your nine-year-old to do his laundry. On one hand, you want your child to gain life skills. On the other hand, he might damage his clothing, wasting your hard-earned money. The best win-win outcome might be teaching your nine-year-old how to launder his play clothes. In that outcome, the worst-case scenario might be that all his play clothes turn pink or shrink. That might be a price worth paying if the outcome is that your nine-year-old will eventually be doing his laundry.

At first glance, it might seem that the only options are: a) teach a nine-year-old how to do laundry, and risk him ruining all his clothes, or b) don't teach a nine-year-old how to do laundry, and he will not ruin all his clothes. However, there is always an additional option. Propose a solution and participate in the design of your future.

Emotional discomfort is unnecessary and is usually associated with feelings of anxiety, fear, uncertainty, and even failure. Journaling was my mirror—it's where I told the truth. When I read my journal entries, I saw my true self. I had no reason to lie to a stack of bound, lined paper. I yearned for a forum where I could be transparent, and that was the purpose of my journal. Journaling helped me make honest lists of where I was and where I wanted to be.

Unfortunately, my process wasn't as straightforward. There was a time where I had a strong drive to create lists. I made lists of habits that made me feel unsatisfied. I was trying to solve a puzzle. The only problem was that I didn't have the box the puzzle came in; therefore, I had no idea what picture the pieces were supposed to create. That cluelessness encouraged me to create a bunch of lists. Just lists. Organizing information was my best attempt at satisfying a yearning to feel peaceful more often. I naturally gravitated toward journaling to process internal discomforts that regularly occurred, only this time, incorporating lists. As I reverse engineered my emotional discomforts, I learned I had effortlessly designed my perfect day by listing what I did not like about my lifestyle. Just by having an opinion about how my perfect day would look, I built a standard for my life. My big picture day was the only thing that moved me from an unhealthy emotional space into a healthy emotional space.

Anxiety, fear, uncertainty, and failure are addressed by living an organized life in exchange for a positive internal experience. By addressing those problems, we will be creating a map to our big picture life. Here is the important part: No one wants to sow seeds today, but everyone wants to reap rewards tomorrow. It's a common feeling—and it's okay. The key is understanding you will always be exchanging something of yours to obtain the pieces of your big picture life. Henry David Thoreau explained this when he wrote, "The cost of a thing is the amount of what I will call life which is required to be exchanged for it, immediately or in the long run."

The Power of a Plan

In 2012, Katherine Harmon wrote an article in Scientific American titled "Brain Scans of Hoarders Reveal Why They Never De-Clutter." In that article, Harmon makes interesting connections with the different findings of a study led by Yale University of Medicine's David Tonlin. Tonlin and his colleagues took fMRI brain scans of forty-three adults diagnosed with a hoarding disorder, thirty-one with OCD, and thirty-three healthy adult controls. Tonlin and his team found that the participants diagnosed with a hoarding disorder experienced significantly more anxiety, indecisiveness, and sadness while making decisions about discarding miscellaneous paper from their homes. Their fMRI readings showed differences in the anterior cingulate cortex and the mid to anterior insula. The anterior cingulate cortex controls the part of the brain that detects mistakes during moments of uncertainty.

Hoarding disorder can be debilitating, but it is often misunderstood. Tonlin says, "The disorder is characterized by a marked avoidance of decision-making about possessions." Hoarding is not about keeping items you own. Harmon later concludes, "The biggest hurdle to recovery still seems to be recognizing the problem." The truth is that in most problems, the most challenging part is admitting there is a problem.

Exercise No. 04: Taking Inventory of Problematic Practices

What to do:
1. Make a list of any habitual practices or mindless activities that you take part in.
2. Review your list and cross out any habitual practices or mindless activities that bring you zero results or reward.
3. Circle any habitual practices or mindless activities that bring you great reward, in any form.

Exercise No. 05: Defining the Points on the Map

Review the general defining points on most maps to self-defined success below. Define the points on your map to success.

General Defining Points on Most Maps to Success
- Current Location: Anxiety
- Desired Destination: Bravery
- Directions to Destination: Certainty

What to do:
Determine the defining points on your map to success
- Current Location
- Desired Destination
- Directions to Destination

Tonlin's study perfectly displays the power of decision-making. The brain scans showed that people diagnosed with hoarding disorder simply have trouble deciding whether or not to discard their possessions because they are not able to properly evaluate the consequence of making a wrong decision at that moment. If that is scientifically true, then we can assume investing in improving the ability to make a strong decision can exponentially produce rewards.

An experiment done in Israel puts the spotlight on

how mental fatigue can change a person's fate. The article was first published in the Proceedings of the National Academy of Sciences of the United States of America on April 11, 2011. Researchers analyzed data from criminal cases to "test the effect of the ordinal position of a case on the judge's decision and the effect of the judge having taken a break to eat." Using data collected from 1,112 judicial rulings, the researchers found "that when judges make repeated rulings, they show an increased tendency to rule in favor of the status quo." In simpler words, as judges become tired, making rulings repeatedly can increase the likelihood of judges simplifying their decision-making processes.

Point B

The second piece of information needed to use a map is the desired destination, a.k.a. Point B. Your desired destination is your perfect day. By mapping the location of Point A (our current location) and Point B (our perfect day), we can see many ways to arrive at our big picture. Our big picture can be literal or metaphorical. For example, if my big picture is of my son and I playing at the park, that could mean one of two things. It could either mean that I enjoy spending time with my son at the park, or it could metaphorically mean that I want the freedom to spend more time with my son.

You must define success by your terms and then put forth the effort to reach that success. The big picture symbolizes your definition of success. *Ready, Set, GOAL!* will guide you through the MORE Method, a goal-setting acronym that I created to help people achieve their goals. Many factors can influence the potential of our performance, and only after considering all the factors, can we truly say we have done our best to prepare for success.

Through much study, I've learned of clutter's negative effect on our ability to focus and process information. In my personal experience, this holds true for physical, mental, emotional, and financial clutter. If you retain only one thing from this sea of information, let it be that clutter in all forms is bad for Operation: More big picture days.

Equipped with the best options available, I've

adopted a lifestyle that has resulted in confidence, stability, and success. At the end of the day, we are all working toward a life filled with numerous perfect days. That's why I wrote this guide. I want to help people get more big picture days in their lives.

Ready, Set, GOAL! is the blueprint for navigating your way from negative emotions to a life filled with big picture days. You will be combating anxiety, fear, uncertainty, and failure—common obstacles to success—with life skills to intentionally automate your plan to succeed.

Your Map: The Vehicle to Big Picture-dom

A goal is a dream with a deadline.
—Napoleon Hill

Now let's revisit the details of that big picture of your perfect day. Who is in your big picture? What are you doing in your big picture? Where were you in your big picture?

Hold that picture in your mind.

How do we get more of that big picture? Planning. Planning is the map that allows us to decrease anxiety, fear, uncertainty, and failure. Planning helps us perform at our peak potential, allows us to consider the variables affecting our ideal result, and addresses any variables that arise.

Planning also allows us to experience the journey to big picture-dom in the "vibe" of our choosing.

Do you want to arrive at that dream high strung or relaxed? If life is all about the journey and not the destination—like everyone keeps telling us—then it makes sense for us to design our journey to be a pleasant one.

Believe in Yourself

I've learned that one important ingredient for accomplishing a goal is simply believing in your ability to accomplish it. Would it be a good idea to jump off a roof into a pool if you did not believe you could "safely" accomplish that feat? That is one example of how our self-perception affects the potential of our peak performance.

Did you notice your emotional response to thinking about whether you could jump off a roof into a pool? If you believed you could accomplish that feat, you may have felt empowered and excited. If you didn't believe you could make such a jump, you may have felt fear, defeat, and maybe even pain.

To clarify, I'm not saying that all you need to do to

accomplish a goal is believe in your ability to do it. I'm saying that belief is one of many factors that influence your ability to accomplish a goal.

We weigh the likelihood of accomplishing our goals all the time. If we truly don't think we can accomplish a goal, we won't attempt it at all. We are always evaluating the worthiness of opportunities that arise and making decisions based on those evaluations. Believing we can achieve a certain desired outcome expands the range of available options to us in creating a life with more big picture days.

Create a Strong Foundation

Equip yourself with the tools you need to succeed. Ultimately, you only need a pencil, paper, and your mind, but it helps to use additional tools to streamline the process.

What are some tools we can equip ourselves with?
- A clear big picture
- Goal setting techniques and principles

- A lifestyle of automation
- Calendaring your goals

Without a clear big picture, we roam the earth aimlessly, not knowing where we are going, planning only to survive. A clear big picture gives our goals a greater purpose, acting as a vehicle to our perfect day. By utilizing our clear big picture, we are planning to thrive.

Create a map for your journey to big picture-dom by making a list. On our map, we mark our current location and the destination—your big picture. Your big picture should signify freedom. Just mapping those two locations—where you are and where you want to be—provides you with a list of what you need to do to get there. That list is made up of your goals.

After setting your goals, you need to commit to seeing them through. The plan may change, even the destination may change, but your commitment to creating a life with more big picture days should always remain the same.

A Lifestyle of Intentional Automation

A lifestyle of intentional automation means choosing to live life with carefully designed routines, allowing your basic needs to be automatically maintained. This reduces the likelihood of falling behind with life's basic responsibilities. Removing moments of stress can be as easy as automating everyday tasks.

John Tierney, coauthor of, Willpower: Rediscovering the Greatest Human Strength said in an article he wrote in the New York Times, "The most successful people, Baumeister and his colleagues have found, don't use their willpower as a last-ditch defense to stop themselves from disaster. Rather, they conserve willpower by developing effective habits and routines in school and at work so that they reduce the amount of stress in their lives." Roy F. Baumeister, Tierney's coauthor and a social psychologist at Florida State University, said, "Your ability to make the right investment or hiring decision may be reduced simply because you expended some of your willpower earlier when you held your tongue in response to someone's offensive remark or when you exerted yourself to get to the meeting on time."

Many successful people have designed lifestyles with this information in mind. Mark Zuckerberg, Barack Obama, and Steve Jobs all chose to wear the same thing every single day to prevent decision fatigue. When we make decisions, we are exercising our decision-making muscles. We might feel decision fatigue after a long day of decision-making. For us to combat decision fatigue, we must automate our lives as much as possible.

Examples of routines that support a life of automation:
- Preparing lunch the night before
- Planning the meals for the week on Sunday
- Prepping vegetables for the week's dinners
- Planning your outfit the night before
- Planning things you want to accomplish in a planner on Sunday for Monday to Friday
- Calendaring deadlines for goals

Making a practice of keeping running lists will put you on a path to intentionally allocating energy exertion. We budget our finances, so why wouldn't we also budget our energy? There will always be tasks to do and there will never be enough time to do them all. By maintaining a list of running tasks, we create a categorized menu of options from which to choose. The beauty in this is the freedom that comes with it.

Organizing

By preparing the options ahead of time and categorizing them by self-defined factors, we make it simple to design our journey to success. For a slower pace for the next month of our lives, we might choose a task from a list that we categorized as *home*, *inexpensive*, *low time demands*. That might seem like a lot of information to track, but I assure you that it's not. For example, those three categories can be tracked in a list titled "Home." Under the title "Home," we might have the following tasks listed: Redo Bathroom, Mop Kitchen Floor, Clean Out Garage. Next to each task, a dollar sign and clock symbol can be used to represent the amount of money and time it will take to accomplish this task. By organizing our options, we will be allocating our energy in more strategically efficient ways.

Incorporating a Calendaring System

A good way to automate your life for success is to record deadlines on a calendar for your goals using a calendaring system. A calendaring system can include a paper planner, dry erase calendars placed in strategic locations, and an online calendar.

It is also a good practice to calendar multiple reminders for important deadlines. For example, I might create an event in my calendar for my nephew's birthday. At the same time, I will also schedule a seven-day reminder for his birthday, an event to buy his gift, and a seven-day reminder for buying his gift. By becoming a powcr user of a calendaring system, one creates an environment for peace, productivity, and confidence.

To understand better the role of a calendaring system in the lives of top performers, I asked Ada K. Wong about the role of a calendar in the success of her law firm, AKW Law, PLLC. In 2016 Wong was named in Women in the Law—Top Peer-Nominated Lawyers, Top 40 Under 40 by The National Trial Lawyers, and Rising Star by Super Lawyers. Wong was also named AVVO Top Personal Injury Attorney, Top Employment Law Attorney, Top Civil Rights Attorney, and was awarded the Client's Choice Award in 2014, 2015, 2016, and 2017.

When asked what attributed to the success of her law firm, she answered, "It is an understatement that all successful people, including lawyers, are highly organized; and the key to organization is having an effective and efficient calendaring system. Law firms operate on deadlines imposed by the court, the statute of limitations, or our clients' needs and expectations. Missing deadlines or forgetting to complete tasks can negatively impact one's reputation—quickly. We are simply not able to remember everything that we must do and all deadlines. Having a calendaring system for a law firm is a must, there is simply no shortcut."

It is undeniable that reputation has a big influence on success. A boxer with an undefeated record gains an emotional advantage from his reputation—it is the reason he believes he can achieve his desired outcome. Spectators contribute to the affirming environment by their response to the undefeated boxer's reputation. This affirming environment makes the undefeated boxer even more confident, which is likely to result in him performing at his peak potential. We can apply this to our personal and professional lives by understanding that the more dependable we are, the more we are perceived to be competent and interested. Being competent and interested in your relationship with your spouse might result in peaceful home life. Being competent and interested in your job might result in success in the workplace.

Dr. Anthony P. Witham explained the value people place on time when he wrote, "Children spell 'love'…T-I-M-E." If time is so important to people, it makes sense for us to respect it as we do our finances by spending it wisely. By respecting our time, we are maintaining the potential for a reputation of quality.

Slow and Steady Wins the Race

Sometimes our status is *not yet*, and that is okay.

Carol Dweck described children with a Growth Mindset in a talk she gave to Stanford Alumni in 2014 as understanding "that their abilities could grow through their hard work." She goes on to describe children with a fixed mindset as "gripped by the 'tyranny of now'" versus the children with growth mindsets that were empowered by "the power of 'yet.'"

The principle thought driving a growth mindset is that with enough hard work, we will eventually get there. Thinking in those terms allows us to be curious, which in turn taps into next-level brainpower that we cannot have with a fixed mindset. With a growth mindset, if I keep taking steps in the right direction, I will eventually arrive at my destination—whether it takes five months or five years. With a fixed mindset, when I become tired, I will consider quitting to be an option.

When we chunk up our many tasks to accomplish a set goal, we essentially create big, clear steps for our minds. When we believe we can accomplish something, our minds feel confident. Big goals are made of big steps, which are made of chunked-together tasks. The secret to accomplishing big goals is making the big steps look small and doable. When we discredit the challenges in our mind, we empower our minds to believe anything is possible—making more things possible.

We also need to address discouragement. The only way we will be able to commit to a plan until the desired outcome is realized is to reduce the likelihood of discouragement. Chunking our tasks allows us to combat feelings of discouragement and defeat.

Seem overly simple? It's not. We are metaphorically self-medicating ourselves with healthy activities that bring us joy, like playing tennis or spending time with people achieving goals like ours. Feel sad? Do something that makes you happy without fail. Regulate your emotional space. Choose a vibe and make adjustments according to your choices. You'll get there. Just create the plan and commit, addressing discouragement when necessary.

Planning to Become MORE

In How to Win at the Sport of Business, Mark Cuban says, "It doesn't matter how you live. It doesn't matter what car you drive. It doesn't matter what kind of clothes you wear. The more you stress over bills, the more difficult it is to focus on your goals. The cheaper you can live, the greater your options." Living below our means in terms of resources is a great practice for success and can only be done by evaluating our return on investments. Now, let's consider how that influences our big picture.

Testing the Worthiness of a Big Picture

The investment for a big picture can come in the form of a monetary cost or anything you exchange for it, including sacrifices, compromises, and time.

One way to test if a big picture is worth exerting your time, energy, and resources is to evaluate the investment. If I find the value of the big picture to be worth what I must exchange for it, it is indeed a worthy goal in which to invest.

It is important to test the worthiness of anything requiring an energy commitment because filtering our desires allows us to be master stewards of our time. If in testing the worthiness of a goal we learn that the investment will not be worth the return, we will be glad we found out in the beginning and not years into a long-term goal. Testing the worthiness of a goal has the potential to save us energy, time, and money.

Exercise No. 6: How much?

Take a moment to consider the possible cost of your big picture investment. Your childbearing years? Four hundred and fifty dollars a year? Dealing with an angry wife once a week? Long hours in the workplace? Your weekly binge-watching habit? Your integrity? French fries?

What to do:

1. Create a list of non-negotiable aspects of your big picture. After diving in, many people find determining the cost of their big picture to be challenging. If you also find determining the cost of your big picture life daunting, start with being specific.

2. Write down the specific details of the non-negotiable aspects of your big picture life. Is your schedule rigid or flexible? Do you host social gatherings often? Do you walk your children to school? The answers to questions like these provide us with valuable data. If your schedule is flexible, we know that you finance your life with a business or self-employed stream of income. If you host social gatherings often, we know that you live in a home, income, and lifestyle fit for hosting social gatherings often. If you walk your children to school, we know that you live within walking distance from the school your children attend. We can even take it a step further and determine the quality of our children's education. If your children enjoy an education high in quality, we know that you either live near a high-performing public school

or your children attend a high-performing private or charter school. The answers to questions like these give us data we will use to make sound decisions for our future.

3. Determine the cost to obtain and maintain your big picture life. Use the data from your list of non-negotiable big picture life aspects to determine the cost of your big picture life. What is your schedule like in your big picture life? Do you have time freedom? If so, part of the cost of your big picture life is likely, everything it takes to be an entrepreneur or self-employed. The cost of your big picture life is not only monetary but also time and effort. The data we collected from our list of non-negotiable big picture life aspects gives us clues to what it takes to obtain and maintain our big picture lives. If in your big picture life, your children enjoy a high-quality education, the cost of your big picture life likely consists of you paying more to live in an affluent neighborhood or paying more for your child to attend a private or charter school.

In April 2008, Jeff Bezos said in an interview with Bloomberg Businessweek, "I think frugality drives innovation, just like other constraints do." This statement has so many valuable layers from which we can learn. If we are to gain wisdom from all over our world like Warren Buffet advises, we can also deduce from the words of Bezos and Cuban that it is in our best interest to be frugal with all resources, including money, time, and energy. By setting boundaries with our resources, we become innovators that are prepared to invent a way out of a tight box. Therefore, we must always create a budget for whatever we do.

Before starting any major project, setting a budget will tell us where we are on our journey to big picture-dom. A budget establishes boundaries for us, determining what we are and are not willing to exchange to accomplish a goal. For example, if I want six-pack abs but am not willing to stick to a disciplined nutritional plan, six-pack abs may be out of my "budget." The boundaries I set for my life might also provide clarity. If I must eat a certain way to obtain six-pack abs and I'm not willing to do so, I might ask myself if I really want six-pack abs.

Setting boundaries helps remove the emotion from

decision-making by helping us think in terms of negotiation. We must ask ourselves what we're willing to exchange for building a life full of big picture days. George S. Clason wrote a book in 1926 called The Richest Man in Babylon. In that book, Clason explains that the purpose of a budget is, "to enable thee to realize thy most cherished desires by defending them from thy casual wishes."

Exercise No. 7: Casual Wish or Cherished Desire?

What to do:

1. Take a moment to consider if you find your big picture to be of value. Consider if the investment of the big picture is within your budget. What if the cost of more perfect days was the possibility of you not having children? Can you afford that? If your dreams cost you four hundred and fifty dollars per month to enjoy, can you currently afford that? If your answer is no, ask yourself if you think enjoying a life full of big picture days is worth paying four-hundred-and-fifty dollars per month, or whatever the cost is. If so, the only thing left to do is design your life in a manner

that allows you to enjoy your dreams more regularly.

2. Write a response to the following questions.

- What is your budget?
- Do you have non-negotiable terms?
- Have you found a worthy big picture?

If you found your big picture, great! But what if things weren't as cut and dried for you? If you currently do not have the resources to design your big picture life, is it worth the investment to redesign? Would it be worth committing to a semi-long-term plan now to later enjoy a lifelong big picture? If your answer is yes, use your brain to problem-solve your way out of that tight box. Make it happen.

If you answered that your big picture is not worth the investment, go back to the drawing board! Do not fret if you need to go back. Remember what we learned from Dweck about the benefits of a growth mindset. If you are moving forward in the direction of your big picture life, it is only a matter of time until you reach that life filled with perfect days.

The MORE Method for Setting Goals

The MORE Method can be used as a vehicle to your cherished desires by categorizing and simplifying your goals. In The Richest Man in Babylon, Clason writes, "Desires must be simple and definite. They defeat their own purpose should they be too many, too confusing or beyond a man's training to accomplish."

The MORE Method is simple. We will be setting goals in four categories regularly—regardless of the frequency. The four categories of the MORE Method are money, order, recognition, and exploration.

The money category is exactly what it sounds like. We will be setting a goal to increase our ability to earn, control our expenses, invest in income-producing opportunities, protect our assets, save for old age, or increase our net worth.

The order category of the MORE Method is focused on increasing the level of order in your lifestyle. Order will bring tidiness to any portion of your life. Think about the following questions when considering which physical areas in your life would improve from increased order. Do you have a stack of unsorted mail that has been neglected for weeks? Is your desk covered in items that are not work-related? Is your closet cluttered with items that no longer fit you or that you no longer like?

Now let's consider the relational areas of your life that could benefit from increased order. Do you have any broken relationships? Are there any unresolved matters that you could or should address? Virtually any type of disorganization can be put in order. This category is where you will set a goal that cleans up a mess in your life.

The letter R in the MORE Method stands for Recognition. In this category of goal setting, we are focusing on acknowledging people in our lives. We might want to acknowledge people for their influence on our success. Another reason to recognize or acknowledge someone might be to celebrate a birthday or the effort a loved one has invested in a challenging goal. Acknowledging people pays dividends to both the person acknowledging and the person being acknowledged, leaving both with a feeling of satisfaction and confidence.

The last category in the MORE Method is Exploration. A goal in exploration might be to try an activity in which you've been curious such as cutting your hair in a new style or planning a trip to a place you've never been. The idea is to explore, and the boundaries are loose.

By setting goals in these four different categories we automate our likelihood of well-rounded progress toward a life with more big picture days.

The MORE Method in Four Chunked Tasks

Chunk 1: Think about what you want.
- Make a list of goals you might want to accomplish. Evaluate the worthiness of your options. Simplify your list, and pick the first one you want to work toward.

Chunk 2: Figure out what it takes to get what you want.
- Make a list of what you must do to accomplish

what you want to accomplish. Create a timeline for your tasks and organize them into chunked goals.

The following is an example of a timeline for becoming a nurse. The individual tasks are not listed in the timeline. Individual, minor tasks are better listed and then calendared because the chunked goals and the list of tasks to be completed serve two different purposes. The purpose of the chunked goals is to frame a long-term goal in a way that seems simple and easy to accomplish, therefore tricking our brains into a state of confidence. The purpose of the list of tasks to be completed is to reduce the amount of re-processing how and when to spend our energy.

Example of Chunked Goals for Becoming a Nurse
- Research pre-requisite education necessary to qualify for the nursing school of your choice
- Complete the education required to qualify for the nursing school of your choice
- Graduate from the nursing school of your choice
- Get a job as a nurse

Chunk 3: List the chunked tasks in the MORE Method

- The MORE Method will support healthy habits that are manageable and automate life with minimal effort. Organizing your tasks into chunked goals and then listing them in the MORE Method will cause you to believe that your goals are easier than you first thought them to be.

Chunk 4: Direct all energy toward obtaining a life filled with your big picture days.

- By creating an automated lifestyle that includes consistently working toward accomplishing these goals, you will inevitably reach your big picture.

Draw Your Big Picture

You draw your big picture—it can be whatever you want. A drawn-out big picture is one of true power. Your big picture can dictate your every step, and if every step is within your core values and does not harm anyone, you should let it! A true commitment to a drawn-out big picture can be unfathomably powerful.

Whether we acknowledge it or not, we are designing our future—one decision at a time. The type of seed we sow today determines the type of produce we will reap tomorrow. At times our reaping seems to quickly follow our sowing because time passes faster when we're intentionally busy moving toward a goal or big picture.

The truth is time passes quickly no matter what we are doing or not doing. That realization makes me want to take pride in how I spend my life. Each day that passes is one day less in my life account. I want my grandchildren to find the stories of how I spent my life worthy enough to tell their grandchildren. I can't imagine anyone boasting to their grandchildren about my ability to binge-watch the latest streaming service's original series in record-breaking time. I want the stories of my life to be legendary. I want my family to take a healthy level of pride in their relationship with me. There are so many options out there, and I want to choose the right ones so that my life is not left to chance.

If your big picture includes a dog and that is non-negotiable for you, it might not make sense to marry someone who says they can't stand dogs. Or if your big picture is of you being one-hundred percent immersed in jiu-jitsu, you might decide to move to Brazil for a summer. You can decide how comfortable you want to be while working toward your big picture life. Your level of discipline will determine the speed of your process, but what matters most is not the speed of your process, but that your big picture is designed on your terms.

No Shortcuts to Big Picture-dom

You cannot change your destination overnight, but
you can change your direction overnight.
—Jim Rohn

Alright, kids. There's good news and then there's bad news. The good news is we now know how to map our way to self-defined success. The bad news is there are no shortcuts to big picture-dom. We have already mapped out the most efficient route to success without compromising quality.

In Talent Is Overrated, Geoff Colvin studies what separates world-class performers from everybody else. Colvin suggests that every top performer achieves success through deliberate practice. He goes on to suggest that our understanding of the word "practice" in terms of improvement, is inaccurate. Mindlessly repeating an activity is not practice, it is simply an activity. To utilize deliberate practice to achieve our self-defined success, we must first define it.

What is deliberate practice?

Deliberate practice is intentional, repetitive, mentally demanding, and unsatisfying. It is intentional because we are purposefully selecting areas in our performance on which to focus. If we are hoping to become the next world-class Brazilian Jiu-Jitsu practitioner, we might first assess areas of weakness in our abilities in jiu-jitsu. If armbars are our bread and butter and takedowns are a weak area of our game, we will not improve by doing armbars repeatedly. We will only improve by intentionally practicing in areas where we are not proficient. By repetitively and intentionally focusing our attention on proper takedown techniques, we are more likely to see performance improvements.

Deliberate practice is mentally demanding because to gain anything from this type of training, we must focus on repetitively practicing proper technique.

Deliberate practice is also unsatisfying because we are focusing on our weaknesses which offers no gratification. Think of deliberate practice as a gardening concept. The plant that you water is the plant that will grow. If we are continually "practicing" where we are already proficient, we may continue to get greater in that area, but our inprofieciencies will remain.

Using the framework of that definition, we will be constructing a solid foundation for success.

Deliberately Practicing the MORE Method

To deliberately practice the MORE Method for achieving our self-defined success, we will need to address the four aspects of deliberate practice within the MORE Method. We will be intentional with our practice by designing our lifestyle to support and accommodate our big picture day. We will practice repetitively by maintaining the lifestyle we created to support and accommodate our big picture day. We will address the mentally demanding aspect of deliberate practice by calendaring our deadlines and reminders, ultimately increasing our brainpower. Calendaring deadlines and reminders will allow us to preserve our focus for important tasks because we are not relying on our brains, day in and day out to retain important information.

Our working memory can only handle about four chunks of information. A chunk of information is a bundle of information that is loosely connected in meaning. When we chunk our tasks together, we are also increasing our ability to process information. This increases our brainpower and supports the high demands on our mentality.

We address the unsatisfying aspcct of deliberate practice by creating an automated lifestyle that supports our big picture day. We are sowing the seed of success by creating healthy routines that maintain a certain lifestyle. The sowing is the part that provides no gratification. Only in reaping do we truly feel satisfied, but by intentionally designing a routine that supports an automated lifestyle, we make the behind-the-scenes part of success less painful and therefore more satisfying.

Deliberate practice of the MORE Method is not a habit but a lifestyle. All of the tools shared in this guide work as a vehicle to take us to our self-defined success. There is much mindfulness in the design process. It is through that process that we create a machine that will allow us to utilize our highest brain power on command for the most appropriate instance.

See For Yourself

You've read to the end and you're ready to get that big picture life. But what do you do with all this information? Simplicity is key. Use this guide as a reference tool while creating a healthy routine. Reread certain sections that pertain to your current season in life. Use the concepts as idea anchors, but feel free to break rules and ideas whenever it makes sense for your big picture. One of my spiritual mentors taught me how to process information. He always told me, "Chew the meat and spit out the bone." The idea is to do what works for you, and have fun with the process because the process is the part that takes the longest. You now have many tools for use in your journey to big picture-dom. Now, it's time to run! *Ready, Set, GOAL!*

Notes

10. **You can learn from everybody.:** Walton, Sam, and John Huey. Sam Walton: Made In America. Illustrated, Bantam, 1993.

13. **Mohnish Pabrai and Guy Spier paid $650,100 for a charity lunch with Warren Buffett.:** Spier, Guy. "My $650,100 Lunch with Warren Buffett." Time, 30 June 2008, content.time.com/time/business/article/0,8599,1819293,00. html.

15. **we learn that the greatest advantage in a negotiation is the power to walk away at any time.:** Dotz, Tom, et al. NLP: The Essential Guide to Neuro-Linguistic Programming. Original, William Morrow Paperbacks, 2013.

18. **The cost of a thing is the amount of what I will call life which is required to be exchanged for it, immediately or in the long run.:** "Thoreau's Guide to Living More by Spending Less." Business Insider, www.businessinsider. com/thoreaus-guide-to-living-more-by-spending-less-2011-6?international=true&r=US&IR=T. Accessed 18 May 2011.

19. **Katherine Harmon wrote an article in Scientific**

American titled "Brain Scans of Hoarders Reveal Why They Never De-Clutter.": Harmon, Katherine. "Brain Scans of Hoarders Reveal Why They Never De-Clutter." Scientific American Blog Network, Scientific American, 6 Aug. 2012, blogs.scientificamerican.com/observations/scans-of-hoarders-brains-reveal-why-they-never-de-clutter.

19. **Tonlin and his colleagues took fMRI brain scans of forty-three adults diagnosed with a hoarding disorder:** Pushkarskaya, Helen, et al. "Decision-Making under Uncertainty in Obsessive-Compulsive Disorder." PubMed, 12 Aug. 2015, pubmed.ncbi.nlm.nih.gov/26343609.

20. **Harmon later concludes, "The biggest hurdle to recovery still seems to be recognizing the problem.":** ---. "Brain Scans of Hoarders Reveal Why They Never De-Clutter." Scientific American Blog Network, Scientific American, 6 Aug. 2012, blogs.scientificamerican.com/observations/scans-of-hoarders-brains-reveal-why-they-never-de-clutter.

22. **Researchers analyzed data from criminal cases to "test the effect of the ordinal position of a case on the judge's decision:** Danziger, Shai, et al. "Extraneous Factors in Judicial Decisions." PubMed, 11 Apr. 2011, pubmed.ncbi.nlm.nih. gov/21482790.

29. **"The most successful people, Baumeister and his colleagues have found, don't use their willpower as a last-ditch defense:** Tierney, John. "Why You Need to Sleep On

It." The 6th Floor Blog, 19 Aug. 2011, 6thfloor.blogs.nytimes. com/2011/08/17/why-you-need-to-sleep-on-it.

29. **"Your ability to make the right investment or hiring decision may be reduced simply because you:** Baer, Drake and Business Insider. "Science Says You Should Do Your Most Important Work First Thing in The Morning." ScienceAlert, Business Insider, 30 Apr. 2015, www.sciencealert.com/science-says-you-should-do-your-most-important-work-first-thing-in-the-morning.

30. **Mark Zuckerberg, Barack Obama, and Steve Jobs all chose to wear the same thing every single day to prevent decision fatigue.:** Smith, Jacquelyn. "Steve Jobs Always Dressed Exactly the Same. Here's Who Else Does." Forbes, 5 Oct. 2012, www.forbes.com/sites/jacquelynsmith/2012/10/05/steve-jobs-always-dressed-exactly-the-same-heres-who-else-does/?sh=17e045295f53.

32. **I asked Ada K. Wong about the role of a calendar in the success of her law firm:** Perez, Trisha B. "The Best Kept Secret of Top Performers." Storm Praise Publishing, 9 Oct. 2017, www.stormpraise.com/updates/the-best-kept-secret-of-top-performers#.

34. **"Children spell 'love'…T-I-M-E.":** Shockey, M.S., Robbie L. "Children's Aid Society : News & Events : News." Children's Aid Society of Alabama, 1 Feb. 2019, www.childrensaid.org/news_events/news.html/article/2019/02/01/

nine-hundred-and-forty-saturdays.

34. **understanding "that their abilities could grow through their hard work.:** "Developing a Growth Mindset with Carol Dweck." YouTube, uploaded by Stanford Alumni, 9 Oct. 2014, youtu.be/hiiEeMN7vbQ.

37. **The cheaper you can live, the greater your options.:** Cuban, Mark, et al. How to Win at the Sport of Business: If I Can Do It, You Can Do It. Audible Studios, 2015.

40. **"I think frugality drives innovation, just like other constraints do.":** Smale, Brian. "Bezos on Innovation." Bloomberg Businessweek, 17 Apr. 2008, www.bloomberg.com/news/articles/2008-04-16/bezos-on-innovation.

44. **"Desires must be simple and definite.:** Clason, George S. Richest Man in Babylon[RICHEST MAN IN BABYLON REV/E][Mass Market Paperback]. SignetBook, 2008.

51. **our understanding of the word "practice" in terms of improvement, is inaccurate.:** Colvin, Geoff. Talent Is Overrated: What Really Separates World-Class Performers from Everybody Else. Updated, Portfolio, 2010.

TRISHA B. PEREZ is an entrepreneur, public speaker, and wordsmith, committed to increasing her impact on the world by building up leaders and thinkers through a variety of channels and platforms. In 2014, Trisha B. Perez founded her publishing company, Storm Praise Publishing, L.L.C. Leveraging the power of entrepreneurship, public speaking, and publishing allows Trisha to invest in the personal growth of people worldwide.

Trisha B. Perez is the author and creator of the children's book series, The Adventures of Josie & Bud™. Trisha has written and collaborated on several personal development books and guides for people of all ages, including *Ready, Set, GOAL! The Gen Z Guide to Achieving MORE.*

www.ingramcontent.com/pod-product-compliance
Lightning Source LLC
Chambersburg PA
CBHW060537030426
42337CB00021B/4302